FAVORITE BIBLE VERSES

This is the day which the Lord hath made ; we will rejoice & be glad in it .

PSALM 118:24

FAVORITE BIBLE VERSES

Words of Wisdom, Strength and Praise

Selected by Kitty McDonald Clevenger

Calligraphy by Hermann Zapf

 HALLMARK EDITIONS

Exodus 20:1-18. 1 Chronicles 16:23-34; 29:10-13. Job 12:7-9.
Psalms 16:11; 23; 24:1-7, 10; 27:1, 4-6, 13-14; 30:5; 46:1; 55:16-
22; 67:1-4; 95:1-7; 100; 103; 113; 118:24, 26; 121; 136:1-2; 150.
Proverbs 3:1-6; 15:1; 16:18-19. Ecclesiastes 3:1-8. St. Matthew
5:3-16; 5:43-48; 6:9-15, 25-34; 7:1-5, 7-12; 11:28-30; 17:20;
25:34-40. St. John 3:16-17; 14:27. Romans 12:9-18. 1 Corinthians
13:1-7, 13. 2 Corinthians 13:11. Philippians 4:4-7, 8. 1 John 4:7-
13. Revelation 3:20. All from the *King James Version Bible*. Re-
printed by permission of the Cambridge University Press. Pub-
lished by the Syndics of Cambridge University Press.

FAVORITE BIBLE VERSES

Let your light
so shine
before men,
that
they may see
your good works,
and glorify your
Father which is
in heaven.

ST. MATTHEW 5:16

THE GREATEST OF THESE

Though I speak with the tongues of men and of angels, and have not charity, I am become as sounding brass, or a tinkling cymbal.

And though I have the gift of prophecy, and understand all mysteries, and all knowledge; and though I have all faith, so that I could remove mountains, and have not charity, I am nothing.

And though I bestow all my goods to feed the poor, and though I give my body to be burned, and have not charity, it profiteth me nothing.

Charity suffereth long, and is kind; charity envieth not; charity vaunteth not itself, is not puffed up,

Doth not behave itself unseemly, seeketh not her own, is not easily provoked, thinketh no evil;

Rejoiceth not in iniquity, but rejoiceth in the truth;

Beareth all things, believeth all things, hopeth all things, endureth all things.

And now abideth faith, hope, charity, these three; but the greatest of these is charity.

1 Corinthians 13:1-7, 13

THE TEN COMMANDMENTS

And God spake all these words, saying,

I am the Lord thy God, which have brought thee out of the land of Egypt, out of the house of bondage.

Thou shalt have no other gods before me.

Thou shalt not make unto thee any graven image, or any likeness of any thing that is in heaven above, or that is in the earth beneath, or that is in the water under the earth:

Thou shalt not bow down thyself to them, nor serve them: for I the Lord thy God am a jealous God, visiting the iniquity of the fathers upon the children unto the third and fourth generation of them that hate me;

And shewing mercy unto thousands of them that love me, and keep my commandments.

Thou shalt not take the name of the Lord thy God in vain; for the Lord will not hold him guiltless that taketh his name in vain.

Remember the sabbath day, to keep it holy.

Six days shalt thou labour, and do all thy work:

But the seventh day is the sabbath of the Lord thy God: in it thou shalt not do any work, thou, nor thy son, nor thy daughter, thy manservant, nor thy maidservant, nor thy cattle, nor thy stranger that is within thy gates:

For in six days the Lord made heaven and earth, the sea, and all that in them is, and rested the seventh day: wherefore the Lord blessed the sabbath day, and hallowed it.

Honour thy father and thy mother: that thy days may be long upon the land which the Lord thy God giveth thee.

Thou shalt not kill.

Thou shalt not commit adultery.

Thou shalt not steal.

Thou shalt not bear false witness against thy neighbour.

Thou shalt not covet thy neighbour's house, thou shalt not covet thy neighbour's wife, nor his manservant, nor his maidservant, nor his ox, nor his ass, nor any thing that is thy neighbour's.

And all the people saw the thunderings, and the lightnings, and the noise of the trumpet, and the mountain smoking: and when the people saw it, they removed, and stood afar off.   *Exodus 20:1-18*

GOD'S LOVE

Beloved, let us love one another: for love is of God; and every one that loveth is born of God, and knoweth God.

He that loveth not knoweth not God; for God is love.

In this was manifested the love of God toward us, because that God sent his only begotten Son into the world, that we might live through him.

Herein is love, not that we loved God, but that he loved us, and sent his Son to be the propitiation for our sins.

Beloved, if God so loved us, we ought also to love one another.

No man hath seen God at any time. If we love one another, God dwelleth in us, and his love is perfected in us.

Hereby know we that we dwell in him, and he in us, because he hath given us of his Spirit.

1 John 4:7-13

Beloved,
let us love
one
another :
for love is of God;
and
every one
that loveth
is born of God,
and knoweth God.

CONSIDER THE LILIES

...Take no thought for your life, what ye shall eat, or what ye shall drink; nor yet for your body, what ye shall put on. Is not the life more than meat, and the body than raiment?

Behold the fowls of the air: for they sow not, neither do they reap, nor gather into barns; yet your heavenly Father feedeth them. Are ye not much better than they?

Which of you by taking thought can add one cubit unto his stature?

And why take ye thought for raiment? Consider the lilies of the field, how they grow; they toil not, neither do they spin:

And yet I say unto you, That even Solomon in all his glory was not arrayed like one of these.

Wherefore, if God so clothe the grass of the field, which to day is, and to morrow is cast into the oven, shall he not much more clothe you, O ye of little faith?

Therefore take no thought, saying, What shall we eat? or, What shall we drink? or, Wherewithal shall we be clothed?

...For your heavenly Father knoweth that ye have need of all these things.

But seek ye first the kingdom of God, and his righteousness; and all these things shall be added unto you.

Take therefore no thought for the morrow: for the morrow shall take thought for the things of itself....   *St. Matthew* 6:25-34

THE LIGHT OF THE WORLD

Ye are the salt of the earth: but if the salt have lost his savour, wherewith shall it be salted? it is thenceforth good for nothing, but to be cast out, and to be trodden under foot of men.

Ye are the light of the world. A city that is set on an hill cannot be hid.

Neither do men light a candle, and put it under a bushel, but on a candlestick; and it giveth light unto all that are in the house.

Let your light so shine before men, that they may see your good works, and glorify your Father which is in heaven.   *St. Matthew 5:13-16*

A GRAIN OF MUSTARD SEED

...If ye have faith as a grain of mustard seed, ye shall say unto this mountain, Remove hence to yonder place; and it shall remove; and nothing shall be impossible unto you.   *St. Matthew 17:20*

TO EVERY THING THERE IS A SEASON

To every thing there is a season, and a time to every purpose under the heaven:

A time to be born, and a time to die; a time to plant, and a time to pluck up that which is planted;

A time to kill, and a time to heal; a time to break down, and a time to build up;

A time to weep, and a time to laugh; a time to mourn, and a time to dance;

A time to cast away stones, and a time to gather stones together; a time to embrace, and a time to refrain from embracing;

A time to get, and a time to lose; a time to keep, and a time to cast away;

A time to rend, and a time to sew; a time to keep silence, and a time to speak;

A time to love, and a time to hate; a time of war, and a time of peace.   *Ecclesiastes 3:1-8*

Consider
the lilies of the
field,

how they grow;
they toil not,
neither do they
spin.

LOVE YOUR ENEMIES

Ye have heard that it hath been said, Thou shalt love thy neighbour, and hate thine enemy.

But I say unto you, Love your enemies, bless them that curse you, do good to them that hate you, and pray for them which despitefully use you, and persecute you;

That ye may be the children of your Father which is in heaven: for he maketh his sun to rise on the evil and on the good, and sendeth rain on the just and on the unjust.

For if ye love them which love you, what reward have ye? do not even the publicans the same?

And if ye salute your brethren only, what do ye more than others? do not even the publicans so?

Be ye therefore perfect, even as your Father which is in heaven is perfect.   *St. Matthew 5:43-48*

A SOFT ANSWER

A soft answer turneth away wrath: but grievous words stir up anger.   *Proverbs 15:1*

THINK ON THESE

...Whatsoever things are true, whatsoever things are honest, whatsoever things are just, whatsoever things are pure, whatsoever things are lovely, whatsoever things are of good report; if there be any virtue, and if there be any praise, think on these things.   *Philippians 4:8*

JUDGE NOT

Judge not, that ye be not judged.

For with what judgment ye judge, ye shall be judged: and with what measure ye mete, it shall be measured to you again.

And why beholdest thou the mote that is in thy brother's eye, but considerest not the beam that is in thine own eye?

Or how wilt thou say to thy brother, Let me pull out the mote out of thine eye; and, behold, a beam is in thine own eye?

Thou hypocrite, first cast out the beam out of thine own eye; and then shalt thou see clearly to cast out the mote out of thy brother's eye.

St. Matthew 7:1-5

LIVE PEACEABLY WITH ALL MEN

Let love be without dissimulation. Abhor that which is evil; cleave to that which is good.

Be kindly affectioned one to another with brotherly love; in honour preferring one another;

Not slothful in business; fervent in spirit; serving the Lord;

Rejoicing in hope; patient in tribulation; continuing instant in prayer;

Distributing to the necessity of saints; given to hospitality.

Bless them which persecute you; bless, and curse not.

Rejoice with them that do rejoice, and weep with them that weep.

Be of the same mind one toward another. Mind not high things, but condescend to men of low estate. Be not wise in your own conceits.

Recompense to no man evil for evil. Provide things honest in the sight of all men.

If it be possible, as much as lieth in you, live peaceably with all men.   *Romans 12:9-18*

To every thing
there is a
season,
and a time
to every purpose
under the
heaven :

SPEAK TO THE EARTH
But ask now the beasts, and they shall teach thee;
and the fowls of the air, and they shall tell thee:

Or speak to the earth, and it shall teach thee:
and the fishes of the sea shall declare unto thee.

Who knoweth not in all these that the hand of
the Lord hath wrought this?   *Job 12:7-9*

BE OF HUMBLE SPIRIT
Pride goeth before destruction, and an haughty
spirit before a fall.

Better it is to be of an humble spirit with the
lowly, than to divide the spoil with the proud.
                              Proverbs 16:18-19

I WILL COME IN
Behold, I stand at the door, and knock: if any man
hear my voice, and open the door, I will come in
to him, and will sup with him, and he with me.
                              Revelation 3:20

STRENGTH

THE BEATITUDES
Blessed are the poor in spirit: for theirs is the kingdom of heaven.

Blessed are they that mourn: for they shall be comforted.

Blessed are the meek: for they shall inherit the earth.

Blessed are they which do hunger and thirst after righteousness: for they shall be filled.

Blessed are the merciful: for they shall obtain mercy.

Blessed are the pure in heart: for they shall see God.

Blessed are the peacemakers: for they shall be called the children of God.

Blessed are they which are persecuted for righteousness' sake: for theirs is the kingdom of heaven.

Blessed are ye, when men shall revile you, and persecute you, and shall say all manner of evil against you falsely, for my sake.

Rejoice, and be exceeding glad: for great is your reward in heaven: for so persecuted they the prophets which were before you.   *St. Matthew 5:3-12*

I WILL LIFT UP MINE EYES

I will lift up mine eyes unto the hills, from whence cometh my help.

My help cometh from the Lord, which made heaven and earth.

He will not suffer thy foot to be moved: he that keepeth thee will not slumber.

Behold, he that keepeth Israel shall neither slumber nor sleep.

The Lord is thy keeper: the Lord is thy shade upon thy right hand.

The sun shall not smite thee by day, nor the moon by night.

The Lord shall preserve thee from all evil: he shall preserve thy soul.

The Lord shall preserve thy going out and thy coming in from this time forth, and even for evermore. *Psalm 121*

Blessed
are the peacemakers:

for
they shall be called
the children
of God.

THE LEAST OF THESE

Then shall the King say unto them on his right hand, Come, ye blessed of my Father, inherit the kingdom prepared for you from the foundation of the world:

For I was an hungred, and ye gave me meat: I was thirsty, and ye gave me drink: I was a stranger, and ye took me in:

Naked, and ye clothed me: I was sick, and ye visited me: I was in prison, and ye came unto me.

Then shall the righteous answer him, saying, Lord, when saw we thee an hungred, and fed thee? or thirsty, and gave thee drink?

When saw we thee a stranger, and took thee in? or naked, and clothed thee?

Or when saw we thee sick, or in prison, and came unto thee?

And the King shall answer and say unto them, Verily I say unto you, Inasmuch as ye have done it unto one of the least of these my brethren, ye have done it unto me.   *St. Matthew 25:34-40*

ASK, AND IT SHALL BE GIVEN

Ask, and it shall be given you; seek, and ye shall find; knock, and it shall be opened unto you:

For every one that asketh receiveth; and he that seeketh findeth; and to him that knocketh it shall be opened.

Or what man is there of you, whom if his son ask bread, will he give him a stone?

Or if he ask a fish, will he give him a serpent?

If ye then, being evil, know how to give good gifts unto your children, how much more shall your Father which is in heaven give good things to them that ask him?

Therefore all things whatsoever ye would that men should do to you, do ye even so to them: for this is the law and the prophets.

St. Matthew 7:7-12

PEACE AND FAITH

Peace I leave with you, my peace I give unto you: not as the world giveth, give I unto you. Let not your heart be troubled, neither let it be afraid.

St. John 14:27

23

THE LORD IS MY SHEPHERD

The Lord is my shepherd; I shall not want.

He maketh me to lie down in green pastures: he leadeth me beside the still waters.

He restoreth my soul: he leadeth me in the paths of righteousness for his name's sake.

Yea, though I walk through the valley of the shadow of death, I will fear no evil: for thou art with me; thy rod and thy staff they comfort me.

Thou preparest a table before me in the presence of mine enemies: thou anointest my head with oil; my cup runneth over.

Surely goodness and mercy shall follow me all the days of my life: and I will dwell in the house of the Lord for ever.   *Psalm 23*

JOY COMETH

...Weeping may endure for a night, but joy cometh in the morning.   *Psalm 30:5*

I will lift up
mine eyes unto
the
hills,
from whence
cometh my help.
My help cometh
from the Lord,
which made
heaven and earth.

GOD SHALL HEAR

As for me, I will call upon God; and the Lord shall save me.

Evening, and morning, and at noon, will I pray, and cry aloud: and he shall hear my voice.

He hath delivered my soul in peace from the battle that was against me: for there were many with me.

God shall hear, and afflict them, even he that abideth of old. Because they have no changes, therefore they fear not God.

He hath put forth his hands against such as be at peace with him: he hath broken his covenant.

The words of his mouth were smoother than butter, but war was in his heart: his words were softer than oil, yet were they drawn swords.

Cast thy burden upon the Lord, and he shall sustain thee: he shall never suffer the righteous to be moved. *Psalm 55:16-22*

GOD SO LOVED THE WORLD
For God so loved the world, that he gave his only begotten Son, that whosoever believeth in him should not perish, but have everlasting life.

For God sent not his Son into the world to condemn the world; but that the world through him might be saved. *St. John 3:16-17*

GOD OUR REFUGE
God is our refuge and strength, a very present help in trouble. *Psalm 46:1*

I WILL GIVE YOU REST
Come unto me, all ye that labour and are heavy laden, and I will give you rest.

Take my yoke upon you, and learn of me; for I am meek and lowly in heart: and ye shall find rest unto your souls.

For my yoke is easy, and my burden is light. *St. Matthew 11:28-30*

TRUST IN THE LORD

...Forget not my law; but let thine heart keep my commandments:

For length of days, and long life, and peace, shall they add to thee.

Let not mercy and truth forsake thee: bind them about thy neck; write them upon the table of thine heart:

So shalt thou find favour and good understanding in the sight of God and man.

Trust in the Lord with all thine heart; and lean not unto thine own understanding.

In all thy ways acknowledge him, and he shall direct thy paths. *Proverbs 3 : 1 - 6*

BE OF GOOD COMFORT

...Be perfect, be of good comfort, be of one mind, live in peace; and the God of love and peace shall be with you. *2 Corinthians 13 : 11*

Come unto me, all ye that labour and are heavy laden, and I will give you rest.

WAIT ON THE LORD

The Lord is my light and my salvation; whom shall I fear? the Lord is the strength of my life; of whom shall I be afraid?

One thing have I desired of the Lord, that will I seek after; that I may dwell in the house of the Lord all the days of my life, to behold the beauty of the Lord, and to enquire in his temple.

For in the time of trouble he shall hide me in his pavilion: in the secret of his tabernacle shall he hide me; he shall set me up upon a rock.

And now shall mine head be lifted up above mine enemies round about me: therefore will I offer in his tabernacle sacrifices of joy; I will sing, yea, I will sing praises unto the Lord.

I had fainted, unless I had believed to see the goodness of the Lord in the land of the living.

Wait on the Lord: be of good courage, and he shall strengthen thine heart: wait, I say, on the Lord. *Psalm 27:1, 4-6, 13-14*

THE KING OF GLORY

The earth is the Lord's, and the fulness thereof; the world, and they that dwell therein.

For he hath founded it upon the seas, and established it upon the floods.

Who shall ascend into the hill of the Lord? or who shall stand in his holy place?

He that hath clean hands, and a pure heart; who hath not lifted up his soul unto vanity, nor sworn deceitfully.

He shall receive the blessing from the Lord, and righteousness from the God of his salvation.

This is the generation of them that seek him, that seek thy face, O Jacob.

Lift up your heads, O ye gates; and be ye lift up, ye everlasting doors; and the King of glory shall come in.

Who is this King of glory? The Lord of hosts, he is the King of glory. *Psalm 24 : 1 - 7, 10*

PRAISE

THIS IS THE DAY
This is the day which the Lord hath made; we will rejoice and be glad in it.

Blessed be he that cometh in the name of the Lord: we have blessed you out of the house of the Lord. *Psalm 118:24, 26*

SING UNTO THE LORD
O come, let us sing unto the Lord: let us make a joyful noise to the rock of our salvation.

Let us come before his presence with thanksgiving, and make a joyful noise unto him with psalms.

For the Lord is a great God, and a great King above all gods.

In his hand are the deep places of the earth: the strength of the hills is his also.

The sea is his, and he made it: and his hands formed the dry land.

O come, let us worship and bow down: let us kneel before the Lord our maker.

For he is our God; and we are the people of his pasture, and the sheep of his hand.... *Psalm 95:1-7*

Lift up your heads, O ye gates; and be ye lift up, ye everlasting doors; and the King of glory shall come in.

THE LORD'S PRAYER

After this manner therefore pray ye: Our Father which art in heaven, Hallowed be thy name.

Thy kingdom come. Thy will be done in earth, as it is in heaven.

Give us this day our daily bread.

And forgive us our debts, as we forgive our debtors.

And lead us not into temptation, but deliver us from evil: For thine is the kingdom, and the power, and the glory, for ever. Amen.

For if ye forgive men their trespasses, your heavenly Father will also forgive you:

But if ye forgive not men their trespasses, neither will your Father forgive your trespasses.

St. Matthew 6:9-15

THE LORD REIGNETH

Sing unto the Lord, all the earth; shew forth from day to day his salvation.

Declare his glory among the heathen; his marvellous works among all nations.

For great is the Lord, and greatly to be praised: he also is to be feared above all gods.

For all the gods of the people are idols: but the Lord made the heavens.

Glory and honour are in his presence; strength and gladness are in his place.

Give unto the Lord, ye kindreds of the people, give unto the Lord glory and strength.

Give unto the Lord the glory due unto his name: bring an offering, and come before him: worship the Lord in the beauty of holiness.

Fear before him, all the earth: the world also shall be stable, that it be not moved.

Let the heavens be glad, and let the earth rejoice: and let men say among the nations, The Lord reigneth.

Let the sea roar, and the fulness thereof: let the fields rejoice, and all that is therein.

Then shall the trees of the wood sing out at the presence of the Lord, because he cometh to judge the earth.

O give thanks unto the Lord; for he is good; for his mercy endureth for ever.

1 Chronicles 16:23-34

PRAISE THE LORD

Praise ye the Lord. Praise, O ye servants of the Lord, praise the name of the Lord.

Blessed be the name of the Lord from this time forth and for evermore.

From the rising of the sun unto the going down of the same the Lord's name is to be praised.

The Lord is high above all nations, and his glory above the heavens.

Who is like unto the Lord our God, who dwelleth on high,

Who humbleth himself to behold the things that are in heaven, and in the earth!

He raiseth up the poor out of the dust, and lifteth the needy out of the dunghill;

That he may set him with princes, even with the princes of his people.

He maketh the barren woman to keep house, and to be a joyful mother of children. Praise ye the Lord. *Psalm 113*

For thine

is

the kingdom,

and

the power,

and the glory,

for ever.

AMEN.

INTO HIS GATES

Make a joyful noise unto the Lord, all ye lands.

Serve the Lord with gladness: come before his presence with singing.

Know ye that the Lord he is God: it is he that hath made us, and not we ourselves; we are his people, and the sheep of his pasture.

Enter into his gates with thanksgiving, and into his courts with praise: be thankful unto him, and bless his name.

For the Lord is good; his mercy is everlasting; and his truth endureth to all generations.

Psalm 100

GIVE THANKS

O give thanks unto the Lord; for he is good: for his mercy endureth for ever.

O give thanks unto the God of gods: for his mercy endureth for ever.　　　*Psalm 136:1-2*

THINE IS THE MAJESTY

...Blessed be thou, Lord God of Israel our father, for ever and ever.

Thine, O Lord, is the greatness, and the power, and the glory, and the victory, and the majesty: for all that is in the heaven and in the earth is thine; thine is the kingdom, O Lord, and thou art exalted as head above all.

Both riches and honour come of thee, and thou reignest over all; and in thine hand is power and might; and in thine hand it is to make great, and to give strength unto all.

Now therefore, our God, we thank thee, and praise thy glorious name.   *1 Chronicles 29:10-13*

THE FULNESS OF JOY

Thou wilt shew me the path of life: in thy presence is fulness of joy; at thy right hand there are pleasures for evermore.   *Psalm 16:11*

ACCORDING TO HIS GREATNESS

Praise ye the Lord. Praise God in his sanctuary: praise him in the firmament of his power.

Praise him for his mighty acts: praise him according to his excellent greatness.

Praise him with the sound of the trumpet: praise him with the psaltery and harp.

Praise him with the timbrel and dance: praise him with stringed instruments and organs.

Praise him upon the loud cymbals: praise him upon the high sounding cymbals.

Let every thing that hath breath praise the Lord. Praise ye the Lord.   *Psalm 150*

LET THE NATIONS BE GLAD

God be merciful unto us, and bless us; and cause his face to shine upon us.

That thy way may be known upon earth, thy saving health among all nations.

Let the people praise thee, O God; let all the people praise thee.

O let the nations be glad and sing for joy: for thou shalt judge the people righteously, and govern the nations upon earth.   *Psalm 67:1-4*

Make a joyful noise

unto the Lord,
all ye lands.
Serve the Lord
with gladness :
come before his presence
with singing.

BLESS THE LORD

Bless the Lord, O my soul: and all that is within me, bless his holy name.

Bless the Lord, O my soul, and forget not all his benefits:

Who forgiveth all thine iniquities; who healeth all thy diseases;

Who redeemeth thy life from destruction; who crowneth thee with lovingkindness and tender mercies;

Who satisfieth thy mouth with good things; so that thy youth is renewed like the eagle's.

The Lord executeth righteousness and judgment for all that are oppressed.

He made known his ways unto Moses, his acts unto the children of Israel.

The Lord is merciful and gracious, slow to anger, and plenteous in mercy.

He will not always chide: neither will he keep his anger for ever.

He hath not dealt with us after our sins; nor rewarded us according to our iniquities.

For as the heaven is high above the earth, so great is his mercy toward them that fear him.

As far as the east is from the west, so far hath he removed our transgressions from us.

Like as a father pitieth his children, so the Lord pitieth them that fear him.

For he knoweth our frame; he remembereth that we are dust.

As for man, his days are as grass: as a flower of the field, so he flourisheth.

For the wind passeth over it, and it is gone; and the place thereof shall know it no more.

But the mercy of the Lord is from everlasting to everlasting upon them that fear him, and his righteousness unto children's children;

To such as keep his covenant, and to those that remember his commandments to do them.

The Lord hath prepared his throne in the heavens; and his kingdom ruleth over all.

Bless the Lord, ye his angels, that excel in strength, that do his commandments, hearkening unto the voice of his word.

Bless ye the Lord, all ye his hosts; ye ministers of his, that do his pleasure.

Bless the Lord, all his works in all places of his dominion: bless the Lord, O my soul.   *Psalm 103*

And the peace of God, which passeth all understanding, shall keep your hearts and minds through Christ Jesus.

PHILIPPIANS 4:7

REJOICE

Rejoice in the Lord alway: and again I say, Rejoice.

Let your moderation be known unto all men. The Lord is at hand.

Be careful for nothing; but in every thing by prayer and supplication with thanksgiving let your requests be made known unto God.

And the peace of God, which passeth all understanding, shall keep your hearts and minds through Christ Jesus.   *Philippians 4:4-7*

Set in Crown Roman, designed exclusively for Hallmark Editions by Hermann Zapf. Printed on Hallmark Eggshell Book paper. Book design: Hermann Zapf.